more praise for
THE BODY HAS MEMORIES

"This Arkansas native will take you on a journey to her arrival in San Francisco that will provide a look into a body's memory, personal and historical. In this tome, she presents us with a cascade of poems overlooking a landscape that seeks to review visceral experiences that hide within the framework of her body's emotion. She invites the reader to fill in blanks offered in her book that engages one to participate in their own body's memory. From joy to the crippling trauma of surgical scars, the suffrages of the womb and lineage for survival evoking personal and historical accounts of what Harriet Tubman and other freedom warrior's must have endured going to battle for life. oliver's work is a fascinating read!"

Tureeda Mikell
author of *Synchronicity: The Oracle of Sun Medicine*
Story Medicine Woman
QiGong energy therapist

"*the body has memories* is an exciting collision of epigenetic and personal history. Underneath the question of 'who(se) am I?', adrienne danyelle oliver unapologetically plumbs the depths and heights of an imposed and reclaimed identity with candor and grace."

Airea D. Matthews
author of *Simulacra*
Prize Recipient, Yale Series of Younger Poets

NOMADIC PRESS

MASTHEAD

FOUNDING PUBLISHER
J. K. FOWLER

ASSOCIATE EDITOR
MICHAELA MULLIN

EDITOR
GWENDOLYN MITCHELL

DESIGN
JEVOHN TYLER NEWSOME

MISSION STATEMENT

Through publications, events, and active community participation, Nomadic Press collectively weaves together platforms for intentionally marginalized voices to take their rightful place within the world of the written and spoken word. Through our limited means, we are simply attempting to help right the centuries' old violence and silencing that should never have occurred in the first place and build alliances and community partnerships with others who share a collective vision for a future far better than today.

DISTRIBUTION

Orders by teachers, libraries, trade bookstores, or wholesalers:

Small Press Distribution
spd@spdbooks.org
(510) 524-1668 / (800) 869-7553

the body has memories
© 2022 by Adrienne Danyelle Oliver

All rights reserved. No part of this book may be reproduced or transmitted in any form or by any means, electronic or mechanical, without written permission from the publisher.

Requests for permission to make copies of any part of the work should be sent to: editors@blacklawrencepress.com.

This book was made possible by a loving community of chosen family and friends, old and new.

For author questions or to book a reading at your bookstore, university/school, or alternative establishment, please send an email to editors@blacklawrencepress.com.

Cover art: Arthur Johnstone

Published by Nomadic Press, 111 Fairmount Avenue, Oakland, California 94611

First printing, 2022

Printed in the United States of America

Library of Congress Cataloging-in-Publication Data

Title: *the body has memories*
p. cm.
Summary: In her debut poetry chapbook, the body has memories..., adrienne danyelle oliver gives voice to being and becoming the whole self. While memory may in its traditional sense be the discoveries of a single individual, oliver is very aware that the act of remembering is a much greater collective process. It is the historical dialogues among the ancestors and the living. Memories dwell not just within the mind, but are made up from the struggles and triumphs of one's entire existence.

[1. POETRY / Subjects & Themes / Healing. 2. POETRY / American / African American & Black. 3. POETRY / Women Authors. 4. POETRY / American / General.] I. III. Title.

LIBRARY OF CONGRESS CONTROL NUMBER: 2021949447

ISBN: 978-1-955239-23-3

THE BODY HAS MEMORIES

ADRIENNE DANYELLE OLIVER

THE BODY HAS MEMORIES

ADRIENNE DANYELLE OLIVER

NOMADIC PRESS

CONTENTS

introduction

:Sage

...of the physical

:the body has memories	1
:#forareason_____	7
:flY girl	12
:food stamp line	16
:a poem about fibroid tumors	18
:this ain't about crohn's disease	24
:4 Mama Mari	27
:ms. Black body	29

...of the mental

:ode to hip hop	32
:school clothes (Asé)	36
:2 sic[k]ids	39

...of the heart

:passage	44
:belly	48
:so(u)lstice	52

:(h)erasure	55
:a day in San Francisco	56

reading guide 61

INTRODUCTION

Dear Readers,

Welcome to *the body*. *The body* here is the collective of memory as it manifests in my life in connection to our historical memory. In reading the words here, you might find your own memories surfacing in recognition of our shared humanity. I feel it's important in today's increasingly divisive rhetoric of separateness to remember our shared connection as human body having a recursive experience. The memories are in sections not because the poems belong in that section exclusively but rather as an entry point into reflecting on the experience as it exists in the whole of us. All of the poems could belong in every section, I think, as I see the physical, the mental, and the heart body as one body. I have the eve of my 40th birthday to thank for finally setting my mind to curate a set of poems for publication. Turning 40 is one of those time periods that makes it apparent that time waits for no one. Many, though, not all of these poems are autobiographical and the rest are persona poems and some are a mixture of both. I love words, rhythm, wordplay, storytelling, and white space—all used with the intentionality of chorus.

:SAGE

Sitting with my pages. Ages from the sages, Sage is burning a turning in my bones. Fire this time feeling just like a jones. Mama on the phone. Spitting these line bout days long gone. Shut up in my bones. Sometimes my neck hurt. And I think I see a scar. Back in time so far. How it get here. Star. Ting in back. Shackling a clack clack clack. Take a picture. Sell a postcard. From the edge of my Black. This universe verse in my past life I rehearsed. Curtain call from the hearse. The words I speak are hers. And hers and hers. Sun shining new day. What my ancients got to say. Use the fuse in me as light. Asé.

...of the physical

:THE BODY HAS MEMORIES

first eye
dreams about church—
now it's not a specific place
it is an experience

I am standing in the pulpit
singing Patsy Cline and Aretha Franklin;
the congregation goes
"ohhhh, chile that don't go" and chuckles

body on pew remembers being
touched tenderly
in places:

head

    "Do you have a fever, honey?"
    Yes, your mouth remembers sounding
    the body's longing for whatever
    tenderness follows

nose

    (nose to nose)

And you knew that your daddy
loved you

cheek

    You have pretty skin, you hear
    followed by a light caress
    Can I have that dimple?
    A playful pinch

chin

    "I love you," he says.
    Before leaning in for a kiss

collarbone

    The starfish necklace
    that invokes summer
    rests there in the sun of June

navel

    "What happened to your belly button?"
    he asks and traces
    the scar with a gentle thumb

Below the waist
all the way down to the feet
there is forgetting

I tap my feet to the choir's song

second eye
My feet cramp terribly sometimes
to the point where I can't walk
No, not feet
foot
It's usually the right
I'll never forget when it
cramped up in a DMV
bathroom in downtown Oakland

I was going to traffic court
to contest a ticket
I got in Pleasanton
for being Black and making a wrong turn
at 7 in the morning—
        those hours when when the witnesses haven't stopped talking—

The officer asked me if I lived around there.
I did, of course.
Why else would I be going to starbucks in my pajamas
I had a perfect driving record
before that moment
In my defense, I wanted to argue
that the signage was confusing
and his white face was…

Yes, in that DMV bathroom
my foot cramped up
to the point of me
not being able to walk
I took off my shoe
to rest my foot on the cold
linoleum
I bent over
rubbed my toes
—curled like an arthritic fist—
I stood up
walked around and prayed for my toes
to stop pounding

with pain
to ease
for my foot to release this ancestral
tension

third eye
you rape me
then you make me love the baby
he got your grey eyes

And his skin pale
like buttermilk
It tough on a mama to know
her baby
born from a man who is
all the seven
sins in his Bible

I try to run away once
sunk my bare feet into mud
a dark brown welcoming
earth
I ran in the rain

with the sin baby I love
in my arms
head buried in my
warm breasts
I ran and ran and ran and ran
until my foot got caught
something sharp
and tight
like a lion's mouth
close 'round my
feet
no not feet
foot
right foot
and still to this day
my feet cramp up
something awful
when I thinks of
running away

last sound
This part is the remembering.

:#FORAREASON _____

a 4-part fill-in-the-blank poem for the overworked and underloved

part one

#forareason _____ti'ed_____
       (fill in the blank)

She is a limitless being. They try to break her. With chains. With words. With the DNA of a heartbreak embedded into her body. Mamma's heartbreak. Mamma's Mamma's heartbreak. Mamma's Mamma's Mamma's heartbreak. Mamma's Mamma's Mamma's Mamma's heart. Breaks. But she smiles and smiles and smiles and smiles. Like a Black man in black face fighting for his dignity. She has to reach way back to the Nile to remind her to smile. While time traveling in between this present and her past Africa, she sweats the transAtlantic. Centuries beading up at the nape of her neck. The year is 20somethingsomething they telling her now. Or is it 1968? Or 1863? She thought we already done been through reconstruction. But her body feels contorted from squeezing behind a whites only counter, standing over her son's open casket funeral, being bombed with her three friends, being shot in her apartment. She forgets what day it is because the lifetimes just running together. And they want her to be on time in this time. To wake up from her dreams and feel like she actually slept where her body lay while her fugitive spirit was in flight.

part two

#forareason _____unsettled_____
  (fill in the blank)

She is a limitless being. Finding it safe undercovers. Indoors. Listening to the humdrum of the news from the TV one floor down. The sound travels up through the thin wood between apartments. Like a popcorn kernel wedging its way between two tight molars rarely flossed, the sound gets trapped between her ears. The building reminds her of TV portrayals of prison. The yard. The motel-like square that the apartments rest around create an echo chamber to complement the inside sounds that seep through walls. Floors. She survives the night only to face a morning window with power lines in view. Gets dressed and walks out of her front door. Leans on the black railing that frames the walkway in front of each apartment. Looks down from her fourth floor apartment at concrete. She thinks: Would have been a nice place for a garden. She lived in a house once. A field. A village. An open forest. By a sea. A sky. A limitless grove of trees. Green. Land. She never thought there'd be so much concrete. And so little land. No cool green grass to snuggle between the creases of her bare toes. No stars twinkling the night. Now all of her sweet things come in plastic of varying thicknesses. Her fingers barely remember the prickly tremble of a fresh picked strawberry from the Earth.

part three

#forareason _____distressed_____
(fill in the blank)

She is a limitless being. She has 25.43 generations to make up for cause "they ain't gone give us no reparations," she says. And wonders what it be like to finally after all these years get her 40 acres and a mule...minus the mule... In San Francisco, she'll need $85,000—give or take—for a downpayment on a plot of land. She has dreams of paying off her student loan debt and settling down with a nice credit score, 2.5 kids and a white picket-fenced budget. In this budget, she follows all the recommended ratios for living. The monthly rent-to-income ratio. The organic food shopping-to-income ratio. The ratio to the ratio for this and that ratio. And of course the ratio to the ratio divided by the ratio and multiplied by the ratio. Living within the ratios helps her feed the piggy bank that constantly asks "Does this make me look fat?" and purges no matter how much it's reassured that a few pounds won't hurt. Apple laptop open atop the kitchen table where dinner with friends could be. She eats takeout next to separate buckets for trash, recycling and compost. She hopes that making no waste is good karma. Wasting no time, she works until she falls asleep sitting straight up. In true Protestant fashion, she feels guilty for ever clocking out.

part four

#forareason _____guarded_____
 (fill in the blank)

She is a limitless being. Finding solace in solitude. Most days alone with her thoughts. Today. Sitting peacefully. All those yesterdays filled up with being open to love. Brotherly love. Sisterly love. Family love. Romantic love. Just open to love. Friends changing. Romance disappointing. Growing apart. Being betrayed. Each experience becoming a brick. Over the years, she'd collected enough bricks to build a nice wall. Now, where her open field to love used to be there is a wall. Her field was a sea of endless green. Dandelion seeds. Full of potential. The stack of bricks she's collected are so high her view to the field is blocked. The wall of bricks, like a fence, stand tall. So, she's decided to paint the wall. A beautiful royal blue. So fascinated she's become with painting the wall, that she's forgotten it was a wall. The steady movement of the paintbrush is soothing. Up. Down. Up. Down. "Hey shortie, let me holla at you!" Up. Down. Up. Down. "Hey girl, you wanna hang out sometime?" Up. Down. Up. Down. "This your Mama! Your cousin been trying to call you, girl." Up. Down. Up. Down. She moves slowly, steadily across the wall, aiming to cover every inch. It's not a wall anymore. Issa Canvas. And it's keeping her beautifully occupied. She can't remember why she'd never had the wall in the first place. From birth. Then none of the bad things would've happened that helped her build the wall in the first place.

#forareason _____
(fill in the blank)

#forareason _____
(fill in the blank)

:fIY GIRL

Sitting on the wooden park bench—
Temperature dropping around us;
i didn't notice i had chill bumps until
You said i was getting cold
and You pointed at my thighs

We were sitting down after a stroll around the lake
during which a passerby had interjected himself into our moment:

You smoke weed brother?
You don't?

We kept walking
while the sunset loomed pink and blue
over an algae-edged lake
you had a smooth, clean-shaven head
your caramel skin as smooth as the sunset

Why all black men gotta smoke
i probe You later in the walk

Nah, he just didn't know
You say

He know
i respond

i find out **Y**ou're full of buzzwords
on this date, our third one

Not real quote unquote Black psychology
like **Y**ou said on our first date

Mamma says later on the phone
i sound tired

Stop worrying about the house
Get some rest
Call the realtor tomorrow
Have a glass of champagne

It ain't the house though

You have to call and talk to your realtor
it's the only way you're going to sell the house

"the house" is the last thing
with a cemented foundation
connecting me to my past

i told You about it on our second date
You asked me how much plane tickets to Arkansas were
to help me fix the house
You paid for our Thai food with Your "Jackson Construction" credit card
i was warming up to You

On our third date,
i noticed that You
wore a dreadlock
around
Your neck;
you explained
that the lock kept you
connected to the style
you wore for 18 years...
i did not understand

After a phone conversation
the fourth date never happened

...

You sound so tired
Mamma insists

Stop worrying about the house
Get some rest
Call your realtor

It ain't the house
It ain't the realtor
It ain't enough rest in the world

It's the fl**Y** circling
around my head like
a
little
angst
barely
visible
in the liminal
between
my waving away
and
passersby
waving back

:FOOD STAMP LINE

HEART breaks in this place. I wait in line where the footprints tell me
exactly six feet behind the person in front of me
I can't take my eyes off the cheap suit that greets me
I knows good suits
not because I can afford them but because I used to work
for folks who could
Cheap suit gives me paper, pen
a clipboard to press on
to make sure the social goes through
white, pink, and yellow

Waiting for my number
to be called
I read a book
(ideas between shiny covers
holding pages bound by thread and industrial glue)
supposedly to save my life
I sit here
because Words cannot feed me as much as chewing
Good intentions and ideas cannot comfort me as much as
fullness in my belly

when my number is called
a strained smile greets me
I wonder what it feels like to be graced with a living smile—
a parting of lips and a dancing of teeth—rather than this ghost of one
strained smile leads me to a cubicle
does not ask about my day
make small talk about the weather
I walk behind her in silence
comforted(?) by the assumption that she is doing fine. Like I am
really not. Both our bodies occupying the space
of 99 percent. That good government salary barely enough
to pay her rent
We both walked into this building
carrying a weighted breath

:A POEM ABOUT FIBROID TUMORS

1.

the black woman body carries Afrika
in her womb
and this womb remembers

cargo of bodies
   waiting to be crucified
set free

    the body remembers how the strongest cargo
    knowing freedom is death
    jumped and returned to the ship
as angels
       while the deceived
       with eyes adjusted to darkness
       nose to the smell of despair
    cultivated another strength
    to pray for the angels to save them

my belly carries
           ghosts
           a returning

a watching

        over corpses

                and living bodies—

☐☐。
I learned
to shrink as an accommodation
shoulders
developing knots
from squeezing closed
    around lungs
    pumping restricted breaths

> *when the white lady doctor*
> *tells me I need to have*
> *a hysterectomy*
> *I overstand that*
> *what she is really telling me*
> *is this*

carried over
in a ship named Good Intent
the body been wearied by this
voyage
and white lady doctor don't understand
how an Afrikan w(omb)und stretched
across the Atlantic and
crucified
can
still   bring forth life
can
                commune
        with
hope

I listen to white lady doctor
read her intentions
and her right to vote
as well intended
        but know she will never
understand the plight of
        Mother Afrika to African-American
battered

terrorized
        dispossessed

tearsinblackboycoffinsandblackgirlchurchbombings/
turnedbloodintheFergusonstreets
because it's cotton picking season in
Mississippi and Alabama/Missouri
Minnesota
Georgia
Texas
and everywhere else

☐☐☐。
like slave ship my body
carries: life and death
        rotting carnage and breathing captive
suffers: the most damage
knows: "it"—she—the universal black womb is crying out in chorus.

and the white lady doctor's response
ishurriedsuddenly after 400 years:

rip out the wo(und)mb

toss her out
in a hazardous materials
bag

matter-of-factly she offers black
hat solutions
as if talking to a child
anticipating doves

I have two other options
besides the illusionist's show
                            one.
I can live with bleeding
bleeding
bleeding
bleeding
blood in the   stre/she/ets
two.
I can be cut
with her help   have tumors removed
empty the ship in Amerikkka
"land of the free"
and wh/try ignoring the

smell of death
sweep remnants
of clinking shackles
to corners in the
fields of my mind
but
cotton picking season
is year round in
America's soul

and what harm is damaged cargo
in a ship on fire?
a ship full of cancer
cells
breeding ghosts

still I decide
to dance with the haunted
wo(und)mb on
troubled water.

:THIS AIN'T ABOUT CROHN'S DISEASE

to be sung in the key of E^b (natural)

It all started with an incision
doctor's decision
that the collision
in my tiny body
was too much…

It was the impact of this and that
hole in the walls
that made the
blood fall
bloody
bloody
in my water
down the drain

I soon could not contain
I call my sister name
"Angel…a…! Angel….a…!"
Angel of light
giving Mamma's blind eye
sight

to the blood fall
bloody
bloody
in my water
down the drain

so much pain
when the healing began…

It all started with an incision
regaining my conscious
and vision
I raised my gown
saw the precision
staples in a line
down my belly

In time they would heal
In time I'd be fine
In time they would heal
In time I'd be fine
The pain would be mine

The healing
in and out of time
The pain mine
Healing in time
pain mine
healing in time

Scar tissue sings praise
at the grave sight
the incision
healed precision
is the line of scrimmage
for this warrior's cry
"It's healing time!"
"It's healing time!"

:4 MAMA MARI[1]

I AM a Black wom(b)an
I AM from a long lineage of can do
of keep on keeping on
of "you got this, girlfriend"
I am not your escape
the one black friend that eases your very white conscience

I AM from the former Confederate States
       of the U.S. (African-enslaving) A.
I can't be your forgetting
I AM Black tears not cast before that swine a B(-lack) woman
I AM a capital B-L-A-C-K woman
minus the L-A-C-K
I AM a returning to
       I AM   the original woman
I AM   f   r   e   e
I am not your magical negra
     not your light-skinned, easy to accept Bey
         I am not massa's (home)cummin'
I am not fixing your dinner
               rocking your cradle
               or wet nursing your white guilt
and

I am not leading the soul train line
                        at your eggnog party
and no, you can   NOT, I repeat

                                      can   NOT
shan't   not
touch.   my.   hair.
                                                to see how it
feeeeels between
                                                        your
   white
                                                                hands
I   have crossed   that mason-dixon line and made my hair my own field

I AM a Black w(h)o(a)(!)man
Please pronounce my name right
and put some respect on it I AM from Aretha Franklin
Patti LaBelle on a high note
Tina Turner on her way out the door
I am not your punching bag and I will
NOT eat the cake
I. AM. (a.BLACK.wOMan.)

---

[1] In 1970, Mari Evans published *I Am a Black Woman*, a defining poetry collection of the Black Arts Movement.

:MS. BLACK BODY

I.
To ms. educate the black body
is to tell her that she is black
and not black enough
that she is "too nice"
but a bitch when she speaks up
that she is too weak
when crying from the weight
of pain
too eager
when excited about love's gain

II.
To miss educating the black body
by telling her to smile
when she doesn't feel like it
is to let her peripheral vision
become a blur
to bounce off stares of
passersby
to point where by 16
she has mastered

looking straight ahead
for protection

☐☐☐。
To missus educate the black body
is to not teach her that
her black beauty
is pure

...of the mental

:ODE TO HIP HOP

1.
Hip Hop, bigger than my lover, hip hop
closer than my mother,
hip hop
swagger like my brother
hip hop
power like no other

Hip Hop how I love thee!
let me count the ways
You grew me up
way back in the day
LL's need for love
DMC's tricky rhyme
you always knew what to say
to bring in the good times
Today, I'm a little bit hurt
I must admit
more days than not
the music ain't shit
Is that the same trap beat
from Drake's last song?
Is that the same strip club?

same girl wearing same thong?
Is it just me or is every song
on the same loop?
merry-go-round
accordion sound
same car making a loopty loop?
No, it's more like a carnival
ride, you say?
The donkeys can walk around
and the owners feed them
hey!hey!hey!hey!hey!
Yeah, you might be right
there's more freedom than I think
but that still don't change the fact
that played out broccoli stinks

Hip Hop, oh Hip Hop, can you please hope
a sister out?
I still be needing you
to be that rhythm-filled drum shout:

W   a   k   e   u   p!!!

from your played out school daze
your pill popping, your weeknd haze

I need some realness sprinkled on top of my 8 0 8 bass
to protect my peoples
    from diss/   place[ment]
                 & where do I go?
    I'm more than one-golden-era-night stand
              Ain't I still a woman,
though?
Hip Hop, oh Hip Hop, please hold
  your soul sistas near
If it wasn't for us
  the underground wouldn't be here

2.
So if hip hop is the Black superpower
which one it be?
the ability to walk through walls?
the power for instant invisibility?
how about the power to blend in
with the white no matter

how [it] blight [blind]?
or the power to walk unheard
through our darkest night?

Hip Hop, oh Hip Hop please hold your
sista soldiers most near
for it is us who need you
most, us who always hear
Hip Hop, you my boo
Why ain't I your bae?
Is it because I refuse
the trends of the day?
No boobs, no weave, no butt implants
to date?
no strip club, no molly, no red cup makin me fade?
Just me and my Black body
stripped bare to my little toes
holding it down for my boo
though he act like he don't know

:SCHOOL CLOTHES (ASÉ)

for Black girls who di'nt get they hair combed at the photoshoot

Stop going there
        for validation
put it down
        the magazine
the remote
        the facebook page
the I-G-handle
        the (tele)phone
O-M-G
S-M-H
the phone
        that be our cue to tele
port
to
        1990
I was an unstyled
chile
on the play
        ground
but   at   the end
of   the
day
respectability was on my edges

because
we worked
way too hard
to get this far
to travel cross these chain gangs
and hot combs
to not glory in a rattail tooth comb with some water on the tips
It's a Black thing
you know
you gots to be Black to
understand that those be
universes in dem edges
arrival at a timeline in my hairline
and
Madam CJ Walker (Asé) is watching
Rosa Parks (Asé) is watching
Corretta Scott King (Asé ^{2}) is watching
Ella Baker (Asé) is watching
even Toni Morrison (Asé) is watching
and mama Maya Angelou (Asé) watching
Harriet Tubman (Asé) is watching
[_____] (Asé) is watching
[_____] (Asé) is watching
[_____] (Asé) is watching

all my Black mammas are watching

and the little Black unnamed girl that looks like me

is watching

and the girl from 1990

all grown up and writing this poem

for us

is watching!

she checking for we

not like they gettin a

check off we

and the mamas

they don't like

what they see

they see

the coon

on repeat

the mammy

the sapphire

the jezebel

they see how they see

          everything

but what we be

[2.] Asè: In West African philosophy, an affirmative Yoruba word carrying multiple meanings, including "Be with us" and "the power to make things happen. Often used in libation ceremony to welcome ancestors into a ritual or space. In the poem above, where there are blank lines, it is meant that the reader inserts an ancestor's name into the space.

:2 SIC[K]IDS

for TW, Rest in Love

a hidden track
train of thoughts
drunk with penny
Tootsie pops
cartwheel dizzy
summer fall
double dutching
on the block
a hula hoop
a robin's rock
rockabye my
childhood loss
baby's playing
with her blocks of
memory block

you had the
braggadocious
I had the brains
or could it be
we be both
one and the same
you had the sound

I had the fury
here's where memory
gets blocked and blurry

baby's playing
memory blocks

I remember some nights
getting on my knees
Daddy teaching me to pray
wishing sweet dreams
Your daddy the war hero
taking Six Flags on
with me and Daddy in tow

cartwheel dizzy
summer fall

I remember getting sick
when I turned 13
homeschool educated
no prom night queen

double dutching

on the block

I remember high school
when you got sick, too
then in college
your Lupus
an unrelenting fool

a hula hoop
a robin's rock

two girl bodies
with womanhood stories
one writing these lines
one gone home to glory

rockabye my
childhood loss

bodies decay/the soul train lives on
herein lies the reason for this song
hereby as it is in heaven on Earth
living one life
in u-in-i's verse

...of the heart

:PASSAGE

it's a common story
the girl in search of her father
the father in a lost search of himself
or nothing
either way both too busted by
broken politics and promises
prelude to picture not perfect
family photo day gone tombstone
with a lonely dash etched in concrete
on a cloudy day
this grave got no grass around it
nobody brings flowers
the father doesn't check the mailbox
for the postcards
she sends from the grave
it's a common story
and bone is the only color
secondary to dust
tracks on the road
and a little girl looking through
a squeaky screen door at the sidewalk
listening to
the ice cream truck become

a melody in the distance
it's a common story
and bone is the only color
a pale ivory like stars
in the sky
or diamonds when you first pull
them from the dirt
a girl in search of herself
and the fullness of stars
cause daddy from dust to dust
a smoke already in her lungs
and all she had to do was breathe
to let there be a definition of happiness
filling the air
it's a common story
and bone is the only color
a girl's undoing into
a woman

                        /dub/

it's a common story
a tongue in search of
its mother

a mother in search of
her children and
her body
spread
weeping
across the
visible world
in fragments
it's a common story
and the only color is blood red
dark
thick
from
a jugular vein
second only to
fire
or a heart
passed between
hands
reaching into a body
killed too soon
harvested without consent
it's a common story

a tongue in search of
its mother
a body in search of
its heart

:BELLY

a meditation on loving the scars beneath her shirt

index fingers
>make a "V"
>right fingernail left outer tip
>left fingernail right outer tip

kissing

+

thumbs
>bent at right knuckle
>bent at left knuckle
>nail beds touching

=

a heart shape

made with her own hands
this heart lives over her belly
the throughline is a scar beginning beneath breastbone below her
beating heart and ending at her pelvis
bone
the throughline is this scar
penetrated with scalpel
four times

in the black space
between counting

                      10   9   8   7   6   5

to waking up
connected to an

                                              IV

she imagined that her skin was pinned
to a cold surgical table
her organs fully exposed
now laying here past midnight
she approaches   4 a.m.
like morning
                eyes wide open
palms flat
rising on inhale
then sinking

                index finger + thumbs = heart

hand

        heart

                over

                        belly

c   h   i   l   d   '   s   p   o   s   e

                beginning of

                  loving
                  line
                  down
                center(ed)
                  her

/

right palm over dark splotch
where
ostomy bag
used to be

+

left palm over two dark scars
branded like dice
where catheter for bladder
used to be

=

and yet
she
is
light

:SO(U)LSTICE

She was reading a book on love
looking for answers
at the brink of giving up
She stops at page 41:

*"To the degree that she trusts her male companion,
lying and other forms of betrayal
will most likely shatter her
self-confidence and self-esteem"*

hooks speaks
to her loudly
to the point of
killing soft determination
to breeze through
chapter three
then she wonders if
the number 41
has some sort of significance
something like
a premonition
that after living

her 40th year of
life
41
will be the year of
God's promise
that all of the lies
will no longer have power
over her

the years
the corners of her
heart that the
locusts have eaten—
with the suspicion
that something is
wrong with her—
will be restored
by an unwavering
self confidence
in her rightness
and worthiness
of upstanding love
There was no breezing

through chapter 3
just as there was
no breeze in the
still of midnight
nor the heat of highest sun
only the slowing
upside down
necessary for larvae to turn
the beauty of movement
in afterbirth
a thawing of thick cold
left by night's icy kiss

---

[3] From *all about love* by bell hooks.

:(H)ERASURE[4]

We   the   ~~mask~~ [womb]   grin

                                                          hide our

torn   bleeding   heart

      smile

all our tears   sighs

                                             see us

    ~~the mask~~ [the womb]

          tortured souls   arise.

sing

        Beneath

                    the   dream

We   ~~mask~~ [womb]!

everlasting song

      Caroling   souls

                                  ~~softly~~

---

[4] (h)erasure is an erasure of *We Wear the Mask* by Paul Laurence Dunbar.

:A DAY IN SAN FRANCISCO

notes from the great migration

Now I am in San Francisco

remembering

tracing

minding

my journey from Little Rock

to get here

I forget how many state lines I crossed

All I know is I am expanding

I look around and see

waiting to hear what the city limbs gone say

if the city need my part before I make myself too at home

The tenderloin say it need

   poets

I look around and forget that I am a poet

'till the tenderloin say

    but you are

I inhale that tender(loin)ness

Then I see a woman sitting on the corner

she throw rocks at the street

like she mad at it

   the street say

     she is

    counting up minutes
'till City notice her
The Filmore say it need jazz
I look around and forget that I am
    jazz
'till the Filmore say
    but you are
I ask the Fillmore how many black folks
play here these days
Then Filmore they shut down the Filmore Center
cause they was shooting
    puts me in a Muni bus
I find myself discombobulated
    in Dolores Park
        the pigeons say
        don't feed the white folks
Meanwhile   Golden Gate bridge say "cheese!"
I am here on Mission watching Silicon Valley

Google bus in white folks who hop on a scooter
I remember the Little Rock Nine
I forgot what we won

School's back segregated

now

I remember I'm carrying tea in my right hand

    to sip slowly

The fog say "it's alright to squint to see! I know I'm thick."

The wind say "it's alright to hold tight! I know I'm cold."

I remember the embrace of Arkansas summers

close to my skin

I remember later today I'll be back in Oakland

The town will say

    holla if you hear me

And let me take my sweet potato soul time growing into

the cadence of this new life

I am ready to go back to Oakland now

Suddenly reminded of when Mama afterbirth say

    cry, sister, cry!

a cacophony of sound I was then

    Now

I am standing in San Francisco like

improvisational jazz

forgetting the song we were originally playing

I am here for the 6 million of us

who traveled far to get
here—
Chicago
New York
anywhere—
far from home
where the city say
> *die, nigga, die*

I remember
we are still wading the water

READING GUIDE

the body has memories

Scope of the Work
This chapbook is a collection of poems exploring the connection between present day and historical trauma and memory. The author considers memory as a visceral experience and contemplates how traumatic memory might manifest in the body.

Purpose
To acknowledge how historical trauma can show up in the lives of present day people. There is increasing research to support the reality of epigenetic trauma that is passed down genetically from generation to generation. When one considers this research in the context of an ancestral trauma such as the Transatlantic Slave Trade, addressing and healing community disparities in a way that acknowledges this history becomes paramount.

Prompt #1
Think of an emotional or physical challenge you have experienced recently or as a chronic issue? Consider the historical trauma that may exist in your own family line. Make connections between the body parts or emotions that ail and this historical trauma. Turn those connections into a poem, specific to the trauma experienced.

Representative Poems
- "the body has memories" (p. 1)
- "a poem about fibroid tumors" (p. 18)

Themes
- Self-Love
- Healing
- Collective Memory

Prompt #2

When considering the impacts of historical trauma, it is helpful to balance the exploration with reflections on how joy thrives in the physical, mental and spiritual body in spite of this reality. Consider what brings you joy. List hobbies that you enjoy just for the sake of enjoyment and not to be productive, though production may be a byproduct of following your passions. Make a list poem that showcases what you enjoy either implicitly or explicitly.

Representative Poems
- "ode to hip hop" (p. 32)
- "a day in San Francisco" (p. 56)

Themes
- Joy
- Imagination
- Playfulness

ACKNOWLEDGMENTS

I would like to thank God, my Mama, and Gloria's gun, the latter of which made it possible for Mama to win Daddy and conceive me. Thank Mama for my first journal and being the biggest fan. Thank the barrel of my pen now making it possible for words and page to conceive these poems.

I acknowledge 39. The year before my 40th birthday and the catalyst for finally putting together a few poems to publish. I thank everyone reading for being a part of this journey. Some of these poems have lived in my journal for years. Thank you for helping them visit with eyes other than my own. I hope you enjoy them. They are from my heart to yours.

To my editor, Gwendolyn Mitchell: you are a supernova. Poetry doula. Thank you for helping me bring the work to a cohesive life. I also want to acknowledge Patrick Oliver for encouraging me to speak loudly. Thank you for the support cuz!

I acknowledge The Last Poets, Gil Scott-Heron, and the Black Arts Movement: Sonia Sanchez, Nikki Giovanni, Amiri Baraka, and Mari Evans for paving the way for poets like me. Your wordplay, rhythms, calling in, calling out, sound and jazz give me permission to remember and create memory.

I acknowledge my poetry shelter: straight outta Eastside Alliance Arts Center, Holla Back's Patrice Lumumba Writer's Workshop; Tureeda "Mama T" Mikell, who curated an anthology of our work in which "a poem about fibroid tumors" is published in a modified version; Dr. Raina León, who helped feature the earliest versions of this poem and additional work on San Francisco MOAD's poetry corner website; San Francisco poet laureate, Tongo Eisen-Martin, whose ability to bring tributaries of poetry community together into a collective body continues to amaze me; Dr. Joanne V. Gabbin and Lauren K. Alleyne, holding it down at the Furious Flower Poetry Center and providing invaluable support to poet-educators like myself; the Blue Ridge Collective born from being a part of Furious Flower's Legacy Seminar; my sista Jeneé Darden and my *Let Her Tell It* crew for their support and love; Lyzette Wanzer, curator of *Trauma, Tresses and Truth,* an anthology in which the poem "school clothes" also appears in a modified version; and my greatest wealth—the countless cousins, family and friends who encourage me.

I acknowledge the inspiration for my work: my cousin Traci Williams, who is now deceased, who inspired "2 sic[k]ids"; my sister Angela "Anjee-O" Oliver, who is full of life and support, who inspired "this ain't about crohn's disease"; bell hooks and Paul Laurence Dunbar, the inspirations for "so(u)lstice" and "(h)erasure", respectively.

I acknowledge the Little Rock Nine: Gloria Ray, Terrance Roberts, Melba Patillo, Elizabeth Eckford, Ernest Green, Minnijean Brown, Jefferson Thomas, Carlotta Walls and Thelma Mothershed, whose courage inspires me to keep it pushing on the daily.

I acknowledge the grand-mothers who inspire me to write, my biological—Addie Parker and Gloria Oliver; and my spiritual—Toni

Morrison and Maya Angelou.

I acknowledge The Great Migration and the amazing story of it as told by Isabel Wilkerson in *The Warmth of Other Suns*. The poem "a day in San Francisco" is inspired by what I gleaned and integrated into my body from this history. It helps me to see how deep the well from which my words flow and fills me with tremendous gratitude for the shoulders on which I stand.

I'm grateful to Finishing Line Press for publishing *collective madness*, a modest and mighty volume that features a few of the poems here. Parts of the poem "the body has memories" appears there in a remixed version, along with "a poem about fibroid tumors", and "belly".

Last and certainly not least, I'm supremely grateful for J. K. Fowler and Nomadic Press for publishing t*he body has memories.*

adrienne danyelle oliver

adrienne danyelle oliver is a poet-educator, hip-hop scholar from Little Rock, AR currently living in the San Francisco Bay Area. Her previous work has appeared in *Storytelling, Self & Society* (Wayne State University Press, 2018), *Patrice Lumumba: An Anthology of Writers on Black Liberation* (Nomadic Press, 2021) and *Write Now! SF Bay's Anthology Essential Truths: The Bay Area in Color* (Pease Press, 2021). adrienne enjoys writing about intergenerational healing. She has two chapbooks, *collective madness* (Finishing Line Press) and *The Body Has Memories* (Nomadic Press) that explore this theme. Some of adrienne's favorite authors include Maya Angelou and Toni Morrison. When she is not writing, adrienne is reading or watching documentaries. More information about her work can be found at www.adriennedanyelle.com

www.ingramcontent.com/pod-product-compliance
Lightning Source LLC
Chambersburg PA
CBHW021450070526
44577CB00002B/345